# This Proud Place

# This Proud Place

An Affectionate Look at New England by B. A. King

Countryman Press · Woodstock, Vermont

Design and Production by Guy Russell
Duotones and Separations by Carl Sesto

**Library of Congress Cataloging in Publication Data**

King, B. A.
    This proud place.

    1. New England—Description and travel—1981–
—Views.   I. Title.
F5.K57    1982      974      82-12425
ISBN 0-914378-91-0

This book is dedicated to two New England families. I prize my connection with each of them. My mother is a Washburn. My wife is a Stoddard.

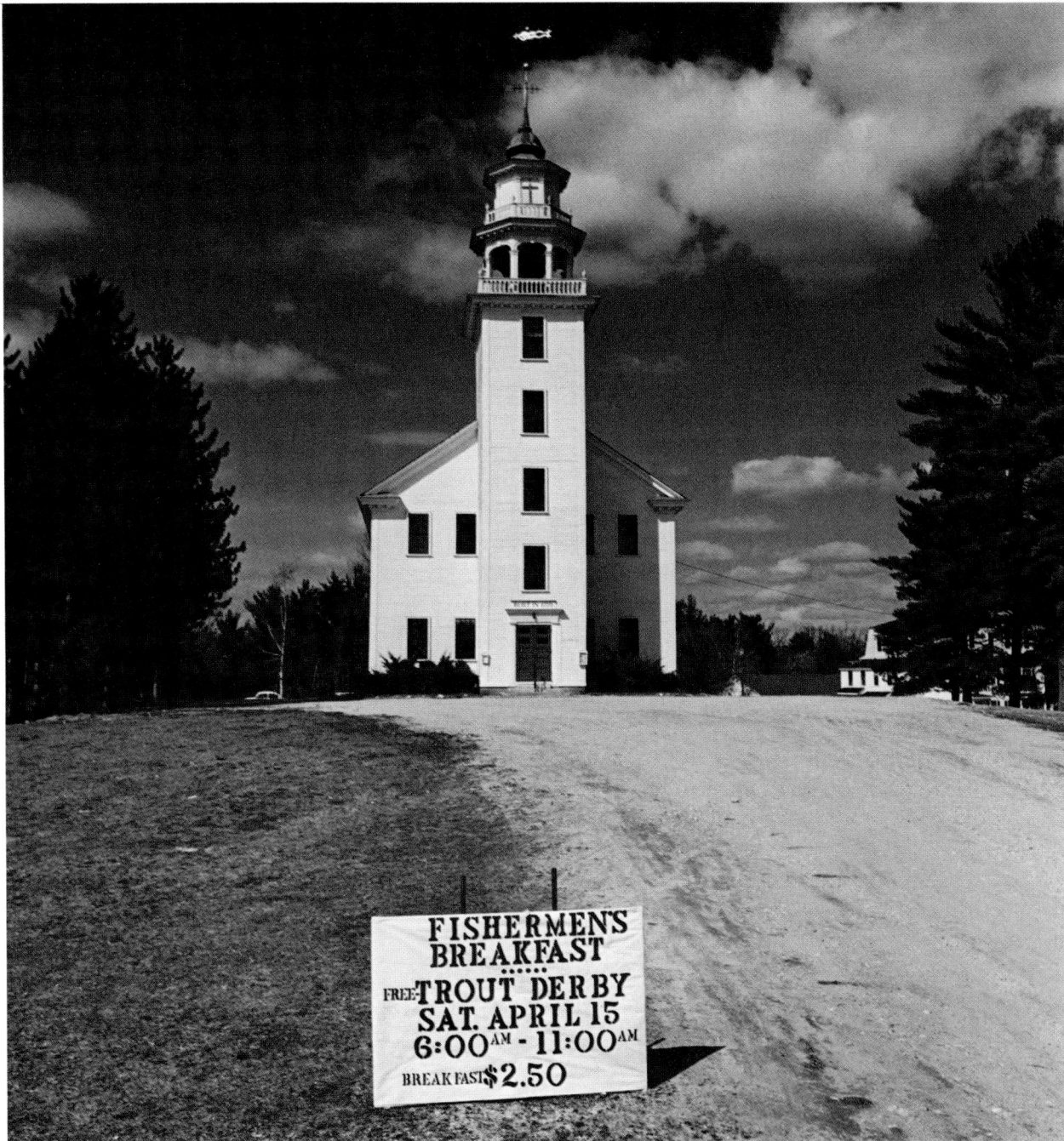

FISHERMEN'S
BREAKFAST
••••••
FREE TROUT DERBY
SAT. APRIL 15
6:00AM - 11:00AM
BREAKFAST $2.50

New England is a lockbox full of heirloom notions and fundamental know-how. People from all over come here to rub up against the hard edges of the elements, as well as New England ideals and values. New England farmers and fishermen are individuals who disdain sham and have a talent for simplicity. They know reefs and stone walls don't change much, while tides and winds are never the same. They've learned to take confidence from what is constant and humility from what is always changing.

New England is a specific place. It's made up of six states; everybody agrees which ones. How many Midwestern states are there, and where does the West begin?

HI THERE,
THIS IS A
NATIVE
ORIENTATED
RESTAURANT
WE'RE NOT
FANCY
NOR
FUSSY
IF YOU ARE,
DUFFYS
BUCKSPORT
7
MILES
SOUTH
ELLSWORTH
14
MILES
NORTH

In New England you can't get away from the sea—the feel of it, or even the idea of it. It's everywhere, in our language, literature, and weather.

Wherever you go you can tell what's important by what people talk about. On the waterfront it's survival and age. A typical comment is, "There goes old man Dagget. He's been fishing all his life." By the sea, old age is a source of reverence, and everyone knows how old everyone else is.

Many fishermen go on fishing until they no longer can. Like teenagers who boast to their friends about how they worry their mothers, old fishermen enjoy telling how their children keep asking them to quit. Each night, two or three at a time, the eldest fishermen come down in their trucks to the wharfs to look around and to be there.

I know a Gloucester fisherman who stays at sea a week at a time; yet even when his boat is tied up, he feels compelled to come down each day to the dock and stand around. He finally had to leave his wife. She used to take him driving up-country on weekends. He couldn't stand it. He felt closed in and lonely surrounded by all those trees.

"The only time I get mad is when people tell me how to fish."—Bud

There are many New Englanders who enjoy living close to the line (borderline poverty). I met a fellow who makes good money working in the woods as a logger in wintertime. In summer he digs clams and picks berries. He said to me, "You are really deprived of things, but it's kind of purifying. Then, just when you get used to living very simply and you like it, you start making money and have those comforts all over again."

New England is wall-to-wall schools, colleges, research labs, summer camps, workshops, conference centers, retreats. There are more libraries per square foot in New England than anywhere else. Education of one kind or another is big business here and perhaps the glory of the region.

This is a white oak and my favorite tree in the whole world. Kestrels nest in it each spring and hunt all summer out of its top branches; red tails have it to themselves in winter. It grows in the meadow behind our house, and our children have grown up in and around it. It's great for climbing or just sitting in. For a few moments when a grade four class picnic was held at our place, every child was up in the tree at the same time.

I photograph this tree all the time, and when I'm away from home I carry the thought of it around with me like a lucky piece.

I once spent a wonderful morning in a canoe on the Assebet River with Edwin Way Teale. He was doing what he called "canoe research." Whenever we passed an inviting meadow or hillside we'd beach the canoe and go off exploring. He called these side trips "small adventures." He seemed to peer behind every rock and into every bush, and he was always touching growing things and pulling off leaves to feel and smell. He carried a little notebook and pencil and stopped constantly to write notes. He explained that he was "picking up sticks." "If you pick up enough sticks," he said, "you can have a fire"—by which he meant a book.

Harold Hugo is a natural leader, a man of vision and a possessor of a divine dissatisfaction with anything not as good as it could be. Combining art and technology is his specialty, and he has done more than anyone I know to raise the standards of fine printing.

Alden Johnson published beautiful books. He was tall and good looking, and his wooden leg gave him the larger-than-life look of a storybook character. He had a towering capacity for friendship and a talent for recognizing ability. The encouragement of Alden Johnson has blessed the lives of craftsmen all across the country.

When I was a young man a Southern gentleman named Eugene Kelly told me, "I can tell by the look on your mother's face that she's never had an evil thought in her life."

Ralph and Caroline Steiner are writers and photographers, a team in art and friendship. I don't know of any two people who have tried harder to inspire young people to believe in themselves and to persevere.

New England cities are physically smaller than places of similar population in other parts of the country. They are served by approaches and byways established by Indians and early settlers. I call them "walking cities" because you can get around them nicely on foot and they are pretty enough so you want to. Even the larger ones have a village green and a hometown feeling.

There's a riddle in the New England character. You can find conservatism and radicalism often in the same family and sometimes even within the same individual. There are stick-in-the-muds as well as plenty of risk takers. I know New Englanders who've traveled the globe (think of the old whalers and Orient travelers) and others who haven't ventured twenty-five miles from home. I asked one fellow about his cousin. He said he hasn't seen him in ten years because he lives "over easterly." The cousin's house is only five miles away.

Hal Borland wrote the most beautiful book dedications I have ever read, and they were all for Barbara, his wife. This is a picture of his house. For me it's really a picture of him. He was an unpretentious and straightforward man. You can't feel his special charm from this picture; for that you have to read his work.

The word "north" holds magic for me. I don't really know why. My natural direction when I have time off is north. My personal meaning for the word is purity, adventure.

I don't like to leave New England in winter. It suits me right here. Some creatures are especially alive when there is snow on the ground. I am one of them.

Any tree is pretty in green summer finery. But in winter you can look deeply into things, and beauty must come from structure. Snow (along with fog and darkness) is an agent of simplification. Snow covers up clutter and debris and has a way of showing things off.

Sometimes I think Queen Anne's lace is more beautiful in winter than it is in summer.

The first snowfall has always been a big deal in our family. It comes like a blessing and is cause for celebration. It happens usually in November, and you don't need a shovel for it, just a broom.

"Look at all the snow. If you look at the snow all at once, everything looks quick. But if you look at one snowflake and keep your eye on it, everything slows down."—Bruce

Nothing makes my fingers more awkward than lacing my skates when I'm afraid someone might reach the ice before I do. I enjoy skating out of doors, and best of all, I like skating on black ice. Black ice occurs after periods of extreme cold when open water freezes through quickly, without contamination by rain or snow. It looks like black velvet, but if you look closely, it's really a rich dark brown. Even when it's quite thick you can see through it. I've often seen fish under it, and once a muskrat swam about three feet ahead of my skates for awhile before he disappeared below regular silvery ice.

Black ice skating is different from any other kind. It feels and sounds different and it's faster. I love the look of the white shavings lying on black ice where a skater has turned quickly.

New England has an appealing, yet severe landscape. The ground is often rocky, the coastline rugged, and the seasons change abruptly and dramatically. You need to cut more wood and store more potatoes than in most other parts of the country. Perhaps it's because life here can be difficult that New Englanders are the way they are. There's a spiritual side to things that is almost as important as the sea and the mountains.